Mainstream Ethics

(ética corriente)

Tato Laviera

Arte Publico Press
Houston, Texas

This volume is made possible through a grant from the National Endowment for the Arts, a federal agency.

Arte Publico Press
University of Houston
Houston, Texas 77004

Laviera, Tato.
  Mainstream ethics = Etica corriente

  1. Puerto Ricans—New York (N.Y.)—Poetry.
2. Afro-Americans—New York (N.Y.)—Poetry.
3. New York (N.Y.)—Ethnic relations—Poetry.
I. Title. II. Title: Etica corriente.
PS3562.A849M3 1988   811'.54   88-6377
ISBN 0-934770-90-5

INTRODUCTION

Tato Laviera's poetic odyssey has explored the geopolitical and linguistic imperatives of Hispanics in the United States. In his first sally, *La Carreta Made a U-Turn* (now in its fourth printing), Laviera acknowledges and celebrates the Latinization of New York, the flourishing of Hispanic cultural values, music and literature in the Metropolis, whereas previous Puerto Rican literature and thought had only rejected the possibility of a Puerto Rican identity on the mainland of the United States. In *Enclave* (now in its second printing), he presents a gallery of cultural heroes whose very essence is adaptation and survival within the enclave that allows for freedom of identity and expression. But it is in *AmeRícan* that Laviera proposes the Puerto Rican, Hispanic, ethnic or minority as the important catalyst in American culture as a whole, the presence that humanizes America, helps her to grow and flourish. But until that happens, Laviera states that he will continue to Hispanize and emphasize the Puerto Rican accent in *Am-e-Rícan*.

Now *Mainstream Ethics* (*ética corriente*) appears on the scene, with Laviera once again exploring the place and language of his people on the mainland. It would be futile to search for "mainstream" values, *pronunciamientos* of patriotic and/or waspish ideals in this book. Our common ethic is this: we are the mainstream. Whether speaking English, Spanish or Spanglish, whether unemployed or marginalized, whether educated or not . . . we all can and do contribute to the common ethic, we can all swim in the waters of that mythic mainstream or we can all disprove its very existence.

Laviera's journey thus began with redirecting us to an investment of our lives and culture in the Metropolis and he is presently bringing us to the realization that our language and lore, our art and history have transformed this country and made it ours. It is not our role to follow the dictates of a shadowy norm, an illusive *main* stream, but to remain faithful to our collective and individual personalities. Our ethic is and shall always be current. Let us make it so common that all of us who reside within these borders can celebrate it, in all of its shades, sizes, colors and idioms, as we search for America.

Nicolás Kanellos
Publisher

table of contents

lady liberty

for liberty, your day filled in splendor,
july fourth, new york harbor, nineteen eighty six,
midnight sky, fireworks splashing,
heaven exploding
into radiant bouquets,
wall street a backdrop of centennial adulation,
computerized capital angling cameras
celebrating the international symbol of freedom
stretched across micro-chips,
awacs surveillance,
wall-to-wall people, sailing ships,
gliding armies ferried
in pursuit of happiness, constitution adoration,
packaged television channels for liberty,
immigrant illusions
celebrated in the name of democratic principles,
god bless america, land of the star
spangled banner
that we love.

but the symbol suffered
one hundred years of decay
climbing up to the spined crown,
the fractured torch hand,
the ruptured intestines,
palms blistered and calloused,
feet embroidered in rust,
centennial decay,
the lady's eyes,
cataract filled, exposed
to sun and snow, a salty wind,
discolored verses staining her robe.

she needed re-molding, re-designing,
the decomposed body

now melted down for souveniers,
lungs and limbs jailed
in scaffolding of ugly cubicles
incarcerating the body
as she prepared to receive
her twentieth-century transplant
paid for by pitching pennies,
hometown chicken barbecues,
marathons on america's main streets.

she heard the speeches:
the president's
the french and american partners,
the nation believed in her, rooted for the queen,
and lady liberty decided to reflect
on lincoln's emancipatory resoluteness,
on washington's patriotism,
on jefferson's lucidity,
on william jennings bryan's socialism,
on woodrow wilson's league of nations,
on roosevelt's new deal,
on kennedy's ecumenical postures,
and on martin luther king's non-violence.

lady liberty decided to reflect
on lillian wald's settlements,
on helen keller's sixth sense,
on susan b. anthony's suffrage movement,
on mother cabrini's giving soul,
on harriet tubman's stubborn pursuit of freedom.

just before she was touched,
just before she was dismantled,
lady liberty spoke,
she spoke for the principles,
for the preamble,
for the bill of rights,
and thirty-nine peaceful
presidential transitions,
and, just before she was touched,

lady liberty wanted to convey
her own resolutions,
her own bi-centennial goals,
so that in twenty eighty-six,
she would be smiling and she would be proud.
and then, just before she was touched,
and then, while she was being re-constructed,
and then, while she was being celebrated,
she spoke.

if you touch me, touch ALL of my people
who need attention and societal repair,
give the tired and the poor
the same attention, AMERICA,
touch us ALL with liberty,
touch us ALL with liberty.

hunger abounds, our soil is plentiful,
our technology advanced enough
to feed the world,
to feed humanity's hunger...
but let's celebrate not our wealth,
not our sophisticated defense,
not our scientific advancements,
not our intellectual adventures.
let us concentrate on our weaknesses,
on our societal needs,
for we will never be free
if indeed freedom is subjugated
to trampling upon people's needs.

this is a warning,
my beloved america.

so touch me,
and in touching me
touch all our people.
do not single me out,

touch all our people,
touch all our people,
all our people
    our people
        people.

and then i shall truly enjoy
my day, filled in splendor,
july fourth, new york harbor,
nineteen eighty six, midnight sky,
fireworks splashing,
heaven exploding
into radiant bouquets,
celebrating in the name of equality,
in the pursuit of happiness,
god bless america,
land of star
spangled banner
that we love.

bag lady

if god were to come
and not be noticed
what better place
than a cold fortress
castle naked street.

latero story (can pickers)

i am a twentieth century welfare recipient
moonlighting in the sun as a latero
a job invented by national and state laws
designed to re-cycle aluminum cans
to return to consumer acid laden
gastric inflammation pituitary glands
coca diet rite low cal godsons
of artificially flavored malignant
indigestions somewhere down the line
of a cancerous cell

i collect from garbage cans in outdoor facilities
congested with putrid residues
my hands shelving themselves
opening plastic bags never knowing
what to encounter

several times a day i touch evil rituals
slit throats of chickens
tongues of poisoned rats
salivating on my index finger
smells of month old rotten food
next to pamper's diarrhea
dry blood infectious diseases
hyperdermic needles tissued with
heroine water drops pilfered in
slimy grease blood hazardous waste materials
but I cannot use rubber gloves
they undermine my daily profit

i am a twentieth century welfare recipient
moonlighting during the day as a latero
making it big in america
some day i might become experienced enough
to offer technical assistance
to other lateros
i am thinking of publishing

my own guide to latero collecting
and founding a latero's union to offer
medical dental benefits

i am a twentieth century welfare recipient
moonlighting at night as a latero
i am considered some kind of expert
at collecting cans during fifth avenue parades
i can now hire workers at twenty
five cents an hour guaranteed salary
and fifty per cent of two and one half cents
profit on each can collected
i am a twentieth century welfare recipient
moonlighting at midnight as a latero
i am becoming an entrepreneur
an american success story
i have hired bag ladies to keep peddlers
from my territories
i have read in some guide to success
that in order to get rich
to make it big
i have to sacrifice myself
moonlighting until dawn by digging
deeper into the extra can margin of profit
i am on my way up the opportunistic
ladder of success
in ten years i will quit welfare
to become a legitimate businessman
i'll soon become a latero executive
with corporate conglomorate intents
god bless america.

drink

what

the

hell,

you

lovely

loneliness,

embrace

me

once

again!

preacher

god bless sister sarah
she dreamt of jesus
drinking a glass of water with her
and said sister sarah that she woke up
and we all know sister sarah's struggles
yes, the lord comes down in strange ways
praise the lord, alleluiah
gloria a dios for our puerto rican congregation!
there's a message for sister sarah
and to all of you sinners of the bottle
don't let the evil ways of satan
drive you down the gypsy road
invite you to the wine cooler bedroom of the devil
do not be tempted
for jesus came to sister sarah
to bring down a message, brothers and sisters
to get high, yes, high with the lord
to get stoned, yes, stoned with the almighty
to get blasted, yes, blasted with the saviour
to get intoxicated, yes, intoxicated with jesus
praise the lord, alleluiah
gloria a dios for our spanish speaking congregation!
nothing is more enlightening
than to drink the life of jesus
one water drink, is all you need
one drink, to see the after world
one drink, to feeeel goooooood inside
one drink, brothers and sisters
alleluiah, praise the lord
glora a dios for our nuyorican congregation!
pick up the pages of the bible
and get yourself drunk
all the way up to salvation
thumbs up to that sweet
wine taste of jesus, yes sir
let us raise our chalices to the lord's words
yes sir, alleluiah

let's gobble up the champagne toast of salvation
yes sir, alleluiah
drink jesus, we say yes
drink jesus, we say yes
drink jesus, we all say yes
jesus is the road
to eternal freedom
come, everyone,
together, lets say
alleluiah, gloria a dios!

some crazy white anglo saxon yale educated
speechwriter got high on some french acid dope
in an international conference of the non-aligned
meeting with the western powers ...
the president wanted a "liberation speech"
to compete with mitterand
to obtain a new base agreement from felipe gonzález
and to upstage castro's inflammatory anti-american
anti-imperialistic speech ...

the writer, high on mescaline,
devised a wasp proposal
which made the u.s. and the president
sound extremely visionary ...
the president announced that puerto rico
would be given independence
as a new democratic model ...

the speech received wonderful praises
the president immediately conferred
with the non-aligned for new military bases ...
the president encouraged the speechwriter
to draft a "detailed plan"
the writer got some more mescaline
and devised a method for the american-japanese
industrial complex to make "puerto rico
a third world economic training base"
for manufacturing mini-parts for computers.

the short range idea ran into trouble
the pentagon and the joint military council
pressured the defense secretary
to retain the puerto rican commonwealth
"why rock the boat?"
"we need puerto rico to monitor the cubans"
"the island is a secret training center for

freedom fighters crushing marxism in latin america."

the president blamed the speechwriter
the speechwriter claimed that some crazy
puerto-rican-on-the-run-terrorist
had given him a leftist pill
that drove him insane
and into becoming a temporary agent
for the socialist cause ...
the president rescinded his original independence plan ...

colonialism speeches were the five-course highlights
during the evening supper meal.

hate

watch

out

for

the

venum

of

its

first

bite.

guerrilla

if it were not for european colonizers, spanish caudillos
sailing to romantic adventures on the high seas,
exploring myths, conquering gold for the mother land,
stealing american riches, torturing indians,
imposing christianity, all in the name of god,
driving natives into the mountains,
possessing, re-naming, murdering, extorting
in the name of the queen

if it were not for the monroe doctrine
big stick intervention, gradual imperialistic
western domination of mexican-indian lands,
colonizing nations, rough riding into
latin america, remembering the maine,
interfering in caribbean affairs,
entering puerto rico without an invitation,
sneaking into its southern borders,
buying governments for dictatorships
in the name of democracy,
at the expense of poor peasants
and broken banana republics ...

if it were not for all of these injustices, then:

we would not have to pick up the gun
to humanize the puss-filled carcass
of your infectious terminal cancer ...

we would not have to pick up the gun
to win over slimy landlords masturbating
on the hypocrisy of feudal promises,
stealing the wages of workers who
have toiled sixty hours on the blistering
face of the sun to find out on payroll lines
that the stinking food and the homeless shelter
was all their weekly checks would buy,
your laughing faces taking advantage

of simple humanity.

we would not have to pick up the gun,
to pulverize your bodies into evil dust,
to burn your skulls, to mame your legs,
to cut your throat, to feed it to the vultures,
to capture your after-spirit,
to rape your soul with evil rituals,
to exterminate and extinguish you with bullets,
to dispose of you in the stinking pool
in which we deposit our wastes
on the day of our victory meal,
when we free ourselves
from your corporate domination,
when we use your mouth openly suspended
to receive the toilet of our hatred.

that's how far your murdering cancer has spread.

there is no turning back,
very little room for negotiations,
there is no compromising.
you are destined not to win
anywhere in the world.
we are the antidote.
we are guided
by universal love
to destroy you.

friend

we came

to hate

each other.

we became

bitter

enemies.

even then

i trusted

that

i trusted

you.

hand shake

flesh

leaves

finger

tree

branches

palm

roots

clinched

two

nations

blood

pumping

adrenaline

reaching out

exploring

mutuality

poet

endlessly
chronologician
wordsmith
underprivileged
sub-vulgate
penniless
moribund
marching
constantly
defying
endlessly
the last is first
the last is the base
chiselers
of letters
relentless
adventurers
endlessly ....

children

        every

        thing

        ever

        imagined

        conceived

        once

        again!

melao

melao was nineteen years old
when he arrived from santurce
spanish speaking streets

melao is thirty-nine years old
in new york still speaking
santurce spanish streets

melaíto his son now answered
in black american soul english talk
with native plena sounds
and primitive urban salsa beats

somehow melao was not concerned
at the neighborly criticism
of his son's disparate sounding
talk

melao remembered he was criticized
back in puerto rico for speaking
arrabal black spanish
in the required english class

melao knew that if anybody
called his son american
they would shout puertorro
in english and spanish
meaning i am puerto rican
coming from yo soy boricua
i am a jíbaro
dual mixtures
of melao and melaíto's
spanglish speaking son
así es la cosa papá

sí, yes, es verdad, we cannot
run too fast anymore,
but we know that if a thief
overtakes us,
at any street corner,
we will not allow ourselves
to be touched.
we will talk mildly
to the assailant.
we will hand over to
the sinvergüenza
everything in our possession
and, if we're walking with a lady,
we will calm all our emotions
bien tranquilito, "take it all,
you can have it, just don't hurt the lady,
do anything you want to me,
we will turn our backs,
walk in the middle of the street,
without any trouble, go in peace,
take it all."

good. he took it all,
but he left me intact,
but i know he lives in the neighborhood.
the network of our bodega, barbería, bakeries
will identify el canalla.
my grandson fights karate,
he went out looking for el canalla's heart
to deliver it to his mother,
i told him it was my business.

so everybody
can rest assured
that any moment now
his groins
will be ground

as basement
appetizer
for
alley
cats.
verdad, socio?

machista

la, tú sabes, tipa esa, me tiene, lo oíste,
la mente, tú sabes, tumbao, con su ritmo caliente,
el estado mío mental está, ajá, eso mismo,
y ella dice, que todavía no le he hecho nada,
brother, me dijo que yo tenía
que coger un training de resistencia,
me lavó la cabeza, me maniobró, me enchuló.

brother, y yo que creía que era el máximo exponente,
graduado con doctorado de la universidad de bembas
con una maestría en labios y un bachi yo-no-sé-qué
rato en lenguas, yo creía que nadie podría
comerme mi coco cerebral, que estaba en control
supremo de mis acciones.

óyeme, brother, la tú sabes, tipa esa, malvada,
semi-y-qué-hembra, jíbara, urbana,
calurosa de su andar, black y qué
english morena, callejera, professional,
buena hija de arroz y habichuelas,
rumbera y qué progressive dancer type,
me salió, y que detrás pa' lante,
en plena esquina, brother, me amedrentó,
diciéndome con sus manos en sus hips,
en inglés y en español y que:

> "look here, brother, you cannot control me,
> so, don't even try, i have too many options
> to be convinced by your guajiro
> back-dated menaces or your semi-jealousies,
> whatever you say, i am not buying macho talk."

brother, y entonces yo le alcé mi lengua,
como para agarrarla, para atraparla, y pa' qué
fue eso, se puso más prieta, se le salió lo negro:

"who do you think you are?
i am living my life at the moment,
i am not gonna hang around you,
i don't need you,
you better be on the ball, all the time,
o si no, tú estás caliente with my boredom,
y si te da la gana de irte, i'm not going
to exprimir ni una lágrima, not even one tear,
honey, i got too much on the ball,
and i work too hard to sit down
at seven o'clock and worry about
your dull inactivities, tipo,

                    ya tú sabes, ponte en algo."

brother, la tipa se fue, tú sabes, enfogoná ...
brother, pero yo soy el machito,
y esta noche, yo pensé, esta noche yo
la voy a endulzar, a atraparla,
yo sé lo que a ella le gusta,
o lo que le va a gustar,
brother, y no te malentiendas,
yo la quiero, en serio,
with my daily brainstorming,
yo le rapeo hasta en english,
brother, hoy perdí la batalla,
pero i am not gonna lose the war.

brother, entonces, la llamé
to take her out,
come, as friends, tonight,
dijo, "yes," brother,

la tipa esa me dejó en la puerta,
al lado del doorman
sin subir con ella en el elevador,
después que yo gasté cien cohetes,
tuve que andar siete bloques al subway.
i was broke, pelao, y la tipa se ofreció
a pagar la mitad, pero yo insistí en pagarlo todo,

y ahora, solo, en el subway,
at three o'clock in the morning,
perdona que te llame tan tarde, brother,
pero hay y que un delay,
y ella durmiendo en su cama,
and i just called her to go over,
y la tipa esa me dijo que, mañana
me mandaba un money order for fifty dollars,
porque ella estaba cansada de mí
"boring, non-progressive, out of style
language talk, therefore i am gonna
change my phone,"
yo le contesté, "out of style?
qué diablo es eso? i dress good."
y ella me contestó que con mi
"ignorancia estás jodío."
me enganchó el teléfono,
óyeme, brother, yo creo que la tipa
esa está loca,
y no viene el subway.

compañero

te digo, i tell you, compañero, mírame bien,
look at what you see, lo que soy, what I am,
te digo, i tell you, compañero, mírame bien,
i am not looking for the moment, compañero,
i am not looking for a fly-by-night relationship,
i am looking to grow, to be independent,
to be assertive, to educate myself,
i am looking for equality, on all levels, personal,
family, societal, i am looking for comprehension,
for tranquility, for dialogue,
i am looking to survive the ups and downs,
without humiliation, so think twice, compañero,
before you think about our future happiness,
you must understand what i am, compañero,
don't underestimate me,
don't crowd me,
don't exploit me,
it is your responsibility, tu responsabilidad,
to respect me, compañero,
and if you do, the treasures of my ultimate desires
will be nurturing you constantemente,
to make you a stronger man
as you make me a stronger woman.
i'll give you everything, everything,
i'll give you todo, all, compañero,
i'll give you the universe,
secretly for your private moments,
and you will give me back
the same commitment so that
we will never suffer from an
unemotional and cold goodbye.
i love you,
compañero.

titi

(To Evelina López Antonetty)

Simplicity stares silently stares silently
Silently silently simplicty stares silently
Stubbornly simplicty stares silently
Silenciosamente:

> We come to seize your breath
> We come to seize your formality
> Nation of nephews-nieces
> Community of confidants-poets-politicians
> City of educators-lawyers-students-activists
> Town of mothers-fathers-sisters-brothers
> Pueblo of brotherhood-sisterhood
> Stronger than ever; smarter than ever
> Generations of godsons-grandsons-great
> Grandaughters-grandfathers-abuelas
> We come to touch you, Titi:

Madrina-Madama-Warrior-Congregation-Talent-Commitment
Determined to fight injustices, oppression
Determined to confront systems, constantly
Unending-unyielding spiritual/physical devotion:

> A BELL LENA-VOICE
> A BELL LEAN-GRACEFUL
> A BELL ELITE
> A BELL MUSICAL SOUNDS
> A BELL POWER-RESPECT
> A BELL DEDICATION
> EVELINA-EVELINA:

We march, soldiers of your commitments
We will fill the vacuum-void-vulnerability
Of-your absence we-will-cross-communicate
To-each-other-and-you-Titi--will-monitor-our
Calls-you-Titi-will-embrace-our-freedom
To-win-to-grow-Titi-you-will-spread-our wings

MAESTRA, how beautifully you taught us:

> Titi-testament tu OBRA
> Tan linda tu OBRA tan
> Linda tu OBRA tan pura
> Como Salinas llena de ORO
> TU MIRADA.

> Te necesitamos, always
> Protégenos siempre, always
> Regáñanos cariñosamente, always
> Keep us on your ALERT, always, always
> We will march to give you

EL BESO, Titi,
EL BESO, Titi,
EL BESO DE TU INTEGRIDAD

> Gracias por tus tantas contribuciones
> Gracias for all of you that's yet to come
> For you, Titi, we offer our HEARTS
> Siempre, always, hasta siempre, BENDICION
> Compañera.

bochinche bilingüe

los únicos que tienen
problemas con el vernáculo
lingüístico diario de nuestra gente
cuando habla de
las experiencias de su cultura popular
son los que estudian solamente
a través de los libros
porque no tienen tiempo para
hablar a nadie, ya que se pasan
analizando y categorizando
la lengua exclusivamente
sin practicar el lenguaje.

el resto de estos
boring people
son extremistas aburridos
educadores perfumados
consumidores intelectuales
de la lengua clásica castellana
al nivel del siglo dieciocho
racistas monolingües en inglés
monolingües comemierdas en español
filósofos nihilistas
y revolucionarios mal entendidos
todos los cuales comparten
una gran pendejá
minoría.

migración

"en mi viejo san juan," calavera cantaba
sus dedos clavados en invierno, fría noche,
dos de la mañana, sentado en los stoops
de un edificio abandonado, suplicándole
sonidos a su guitarra,
pero:
                    sus cuerdas no sonaban,
                    el frío hacía daño,
                    noel estrada, compositor,
                    había muerto, un trovador
                    callejero le lloraba:

"cuántos sueños forgé," calavera voz arrastrándose,
notas musicales, hondas huellas digitales,
guindando sobre cuerdas, sacándole música al hielo,
la fría tempestad,
creando verano con lágrimas,
calor de llantos,
"en mis noches de infancia, mi primera ilusión,"
sentado en los stoops,
"son recuerdos del alma,"
de un edificio abandonado,
pero:
                    sus cuerdas no sonaban,
                    el frío hacía daño,
                    noel estrada, compositor,
                    había muerto, un trovador
                    callejero le lloraba:

"una tarde partí," calavera pensó en la decisión,
operation bootstrap, carreta, barco/avión,
"hacia extraña nación,"
sentado en los stoops,
"pues lo quiso el destino,"
de un edificio abandonado
pero:

           sus cuerdas no sonaban,
           el frío hacía daño,
           noel estrada había muerto,
           un trovador callejero
           le lloraba:

"pero mi corazón," calavera pensó en el sueño,
de cualquier migrante hispano,
nadie quería morirse en américa,
"se quedó junto al mar,"
calavera plena melancolía,
el puertorro no se paró en ellis island,
se sentían short range citizens,

venimos para regresar,
solamente nos quedamos
sentados en los stoops
porque el sueño se pudrió,
en la ilusión de los huecos
de un edificio abandonado,
pero:

           sus cuerdas no sonaban,
           el frío hacía daño,
           noel estrada, había muerto,
           un trovador callejero
           le lloraba:

"pero el tiempo pasó," calavera cantó,
"y el destino," agrio licor
se le olvidó una estrofa,
"mi terrible nostalgia," la gran canción
coros en barberías,
"y no pude volver,"
muchedumbre night club celebraba,
"al san juan que yo amé,"
voces dulces alejadas de borinquen,
"pedacito de patria,"
calavera miró oscuridad,
"mi cabello blanqueó,"
oscuridad miró a calavera,

"ya mi vida se va,"
botella terminada,
"ya la muerte me llama,"
sentado en los stoops,
"y no puedo vivir,"
de un edificio abandonado,
"alejado de ti,"
calavera se paró, decidido,
"puerto rico del alma,"
calavera cantaba:

"adiós," andando hacia el east river,
"adiós," a batallar inconveniencias,
"adiós," a crear ritmos,
"borinquen," ganarle a la fría noche,
"querida," a esperar la madrugada,
"tierra," a apagar la luna,
"de mi amor," esperando el sol,
"adiós," caliente calor,
"adiós," calavera lloraba,
"adiós," sus lágrimas,
"mi diosa," calientes,
"del mar," bajando hasta el suelo,
"mi reina," quemando la acera, carretera,
"del palmar," lágrimas en transcurso,
"me voy," aclimaban las cuerdas,
"ya me voy," y pasaron por sus manos,
"pero un día," y todo se calentó,
"volveré," sin el sol,
"a buscar," y finalmente
"mi querer," las cuerdas sonaron,
"a soñar otra vez," el frío no hacía daño,
"en mi viejo," el sol salió, besó a calavera,
"san juan," al nombre de noel estrada.

calavera abrió las manos en un ritual
hacia el sol, calavera contestó, cantó, terminó,
"en mi viejo san juan."

barrio (forenglishonly)

el inglés
  se desforma
    con el
      calor de
        tu cultura

          lenguas en
            sonidos
              coloquiales
                onomatopeyándose
                  con
                    aztlán
                      clave
                        del coquí

                          aquí
                            el español
                              se coje
                                a pecho
                                  valorizado
                                    profundamente

                              entonces
                                se
                                  digestionan
                                    anglicismos
                                      nuyorriqueños
                                        chicanerías
                                          mezcladas
                                            en spanish
                                              idioms
                                                dentro del
                                                  no-mare-wha
                                                    india
                                                      wha-re-monton
                                                        pitando
                                                          piropos

atoloquedá

        entonces
          es
            que
              surge
                el
                  inglés
                    puro
                      "what's
                        happening
                          man,"
                            in
                                black
                                  english

social club

un "trago straight," cuba libre de don q
y el speech que dice John F. Kennedy balanceado
con el alcalde de ponce, un indio
fumando la pipa, cara pintada colorá,
cuatro cigarros, pote de miel,
museo de reliquias, silla antropológica,
valores folklóricos, barrio urbano,
club fraternal, a nivel de esquina,
en oro plástico, allá arriba velando
san lázaro, su piel chillando
sangre sobre muletas, vellones y chavitos,
por la gracia de yemayá,
se estudian las costumbres,
que son la base del pueblo,
filosofía diaria, narración documentada.

la india en la vitrina, protege la puerta,
velas en escapularios de cocos,
congo haitiano, escultura de madera,
alcanzando a dos mujeres rubias,
con senos apropiados,
pero la negra africana,
guillada en incandescente,
es el afro-centro de la pared boricua,
sentada encima del tite, orgullosa
de su semi-desnuda realidad.

por la entrada del "capicu," "chucha,"
"dóblese hombre," "no me cierre la puerta,"
juego del dominó, al lado del billar,
Martin Luther King Jr. y Roberto Clemente,
observando los mitos, historias locales,
detalles de periódicos, en esta comunidad,
botellas de miller high life,
aguantan antenas, la vellonera es *out of order,*
hoy se usa "el music box,"
se venden cervecitas por camoflaje,

en tres esquinas, el sóngoro consongo de mamey,
hector lavoe gratis, para el deleite
de los pedro navajas, que venden escobas,
hechas de varas para pescar en los alcantarrillados.

en la entrada del toilet
pusieron un tigre,
con la boca abierta,
y una pistola para advertirte,
que si entras a meterte estofá,
te va a comer un alacrán,
una persona inside solamente,
encima de cartelones bilingües
encima, las películas de buck jones, humphrey
bogart, black cat, two-fisted jorge
negrete, revoluces de boca, a cada instante,
sólo quedan maones irregulares,
extra large, los viejos comentan,
que sus "barrigas de budweiser,"
no han llegado a ese extremo.

la bandera americana es solamente un souvenier,
trofeos con palabras mal deletreadas,
vírgenes suplicándole a los machos alzando pesas,
dientes de hierro protegen el retrato de
Rafael Cortijo, el más alto, una escultura de tiza,
en honor a nuestra música,
con la bandera de Puerto Rico,
en escudo de bomba.

el establecimineto rodeado
por cuatro cuadros,
hecho en gold plate,
por una muchacha que firma *md*,
la doctora de fresquerías,
que vende a quince pesos
escenas de tarzán
guindando de un árbol en la jungla,
desnudo con jane los dos *swinging*
en la misma soga pero jane cogió
el órgano de tarzán en vez de la soga,

tarzán con su cara dolorosa gritando,
"Jane, grab the goddamn vine, Jane!!"

en otro display las letras dicen,
EL GALLITO DE MANATI,
vemos un gallo grande,
de plumas negras,
con *psychedelic paint*,
y de momento debajo del gallo,
el órgano de macho más grande
y más pelao del pueblo,
ése es el gallo puertorro!

la muchacha que firma *md*
vende otro cuadro,
Ordenen sus Cerditos,
ahora in advance,
se ve un puerco
encima de una puerquita,
metiendo mano, también en
psychedelic holiday greetings,
dice el cuadro, "order your
christmas ham," the lechoncitos
"are being made to order,"
la puerquita contentita
sudando en "ecstasy!!"

Ismael Rivera hace los hombres soñar
las panderetas, número siete de
la suerte hoy, ocho por uno
tirando los topos, cincuenta cohetes
tragaos por la casa, paraíso de borinquen,
debajo de otra bandera de puerto rico,
y un retrato de don pedro albizu campos,
joven y nacionalista saliendo de la corte,
"defendiendo los derechos de mi patria,"

otra fría, pai, con rumba de Tito Rodríguez,
al compás de una plena, el entra-sale
vendedores de sopa en lata,
cincuenta chavos pa la curita,

un moreno vende wholesale
marketa de lipsticks por diez dólares.

dos mujeres, trabajadoras de factoría,
entran cuidadosamente a tomarse unas cervecitas,
mientras dos machitos de la vieja guardia
empiezan la controversia de panzas,
"tú eres una nenita al lado de mi falda,"
"cállate zafao,"
"tú hablas como el sapo,"
"vete a trabajar pa que me mantengas,"
"tú eres tan flaco que no le haces cosquilla
a un mapo,"
"anda como un gallo desenfrenao,"
a ver si las trabajadoras le ríen las gracias,
para empezar un rapeo.

observamos el tercer retrato de John F. Kennedy,
con su hermano Robert F. Kennedy,
artículo de periódico
con el retrato de Marilyn Monroe,
acusando que Robert sirvió de mensajero
al presidente para tirarle piropos
a Marilyn, mientras Jacqueline estaba
encinta de Caroline. El Papa Juan
veinte y tres bendice todo esto con
la señal de la cruz.

la doctora de fresquerías,
la *md,* que hace los cuadros,
la arrestaron por ser terrorista,
nadie lo cree, cómo es posible,
finalmente se llega a la conclusión que,
como ella era "de la underground,"
tenía que hacer "un trabajo,"
"totalmente absurdo,"
para que "no la descubrieran,"
era como los nacionalistas
que vinieron a nueva york
fugándose en los cincuentas,
y se volvieron ministros pentacostales.

los hombres se acercan cuidadosamente
estudiando el último cuadro de la *md*,
al *road runner* lo están ahorcando
por el *coyote*, que siempre lo persigue,
con la manguera pelá del órgano,
penetrándose en la letra *psychedelic* del coyote,
"now 'Beep Beep,' you sanafabeech,"
los hombres diciendo que los cuadros
"son collector's items,"
el dueño comentando que quizás
"había un tema revolucionario
adentro de toda esa fresquería,"
en el social club,
museo de reliquias,
silla antropológica,
valores folklóricos
de un barrio urbano,
club fraternal,
a nivel de esquina,
filosofía diaria,
narración documentada.

un
vals
en
vallenato
picoteando
samba
merengueada
con
ranchera
de
mambo
combinada
en
salsa
de
plena
polka
rumbeando
bolero
a
la
cha
cha
cha
chi
cha
peruana
cumbia
folklórica
bomba
y
guaracha
picaíta
seis
de
andino
danza

mezclada
en
baladas
nocturnas
de
tango
son
de
unotodos
todosuno
pasitos
unidos
a la
vuelta
del
compás.

conciencia

te hablo porque puedo hablar
tengo la confianza que entiendes
mi genocidio mi pesadilla
mi esclavitud mis cadenas invisibles
mis libertades falsas
te digo que nuestra gente duerme

te hablo porque puedo hablar
porque no somos uno tú y yo
porque no estamos unidos tú y yo
porque no buscamos la expresión interna

te hablo y ahora te pregunto

de qué manera podemos acercarnos mutuamente
que es el todo-feliz que anhelamos
con qué intención existe el pensamiento
cuál verso en la soledad decimos dormimos vivimos

te pregunto y te contesto
no existe tal fenómeno
la sociedad ha roto tal camino
sólo se encuentran
frases mutiladas
sílabas congeladas
silencio desorientado
brisa volando locamente
no existe
un compañerismo acogedor
un momento colectivo para entonarnos
calentarnos porque así es la ley
natural de los sentidos

te hablo porque puedo hablar
porque te busco ansiosamente
por las avenidas del arrabal
abajo en mil angustias

oigo algo que hay
algo que nos hace pensar que hay
algo que impide a lumbre de regocijos que hay
algo que nos achanta el progreso
te pregunto porque entiendo
que tú sigues buscando
dentro de mil pellejos
dentro de la nada del silencio
dentro de agrios momentos
allá en el abajo-biznieto-sufrimiento
muchas veces concluimos que
nada somos ni seremos
somos esclavos del dulce caminar de la pobreza
cadena perpetua
calle sin salida
dolores familiares
decepciones
pesadillas de amores pisoteados
arrogante pecado competencia
ilusiones de trabajo,
el landlord todo-lo-nuestro rata malo
a veces nos apesta
el sudor de los esfuerzos
sacamos lengua al zalapastroso negociante
maldecimos al dichoso olor del progreso
penetrándose como si hubiera futuro
y nosotros fiel compradores
planeando la vida del carusel
comiendo el mango agrio de ilusiones
la cáscara podrida carcajada del progreso
hasta aquí llegan las llagas de la búsqueda
a ver si cerramos los ojos
tan siquiera un momento
a ver si

        un nosotros
        un nosotros verdadero
        un nosotros poderoso
        un nosotros lleno
        un nosotros amoroso
a ver si

un nosotros humano
alzamos las voces
constantemente
al ritmo de insistencia
resistencia
un nosotros crítico
que abre la boca
que no se estanca
un nosotros que declara
somos el mar de nuestro destino
somos la lengua de nuestras acciones
no le tememos al miedo
sabemos que el sin hablar nos oprime
que caiga lo que caiga como caiga
cuando caiga que caiga donde caiga
el silencio nos mata aquí
inundémonos con la mirada fija
con la pelea externa
pónganse ciegos
no oigan la soledad
háganse soldados de su destino
sin parar
cuando pierdas párate
sin parar
habla otra vez
caíste párate
esta fuerza en que vivimos
sólo conoce
sólo reconoce

> la demanda
> la huelga
> el motín
> la violencia
> la persistencia
> la política electoral
> el dinero

la lengua es
la ametralladora
de la libertad

háganlo para el futuro
de nuestros hijos
oigan no se achanten
ganaremos.